GET YOUR FIN.

READ IT • DIGEST IT • ACT ON IT

MONEY MANAGEMENT FOR ANYONE WILLING TO LISTEN

ANDREW TURNER

CONTENTS

CHAPTER 1 - We live in volatile times

CHAPTER 2 - My own take on personal finance

CHAPTER 3 - Income & bank accounts

CHAPTER 4 - Expenses (spending)

CHAPTER 5 - Debt

CHAPTER 6 - Credit, debit & pre-pay cards

CHAPTER 7 - Savings

CHAPTER 8 - Investments

CHAPTER 9 - Net Worth

CHAPTER 10 - Tax & inheritance planning

CHAPTER 11 - Credit score

CHAPTER 12 - My financial set of rules

CHAPTER 13 – A plan for each decade

About the author

Andrew Turner is a UK based entrepreneur. He was once in serious debt. In his early twenties, with no financial nous and nobody around to turn to for advice, he made a series of mistakes which left him with a mountain of debt and consequently very few options. Close to bankruptcy and on the verge of losing the family home, he made some decisions about how he managed his money that would change the course of his life.

From the starting point of near financial disaster, it was not easy, the financial battles he faced were testing and the road to recovery was long. However, the lessons learnt and the challenges that he overcame have culminated in this book. Had he read a book like this, and implemented the suggestions made back in those early days it's likely that things would have gone very differently and that this book would never have been written.

Thanks to the changes he made to the way he thought about and managed his money, he is now living a largely financially stress free life.

How this book came to be written

Andrew was once in a very dangerous place from a financial point of view. He owed a great deal of money. A series of bad decisions, a failed business, a complicated private life and spending way beyond his means - partly to null the pain - left him close to bankruptcy and within a hairs breadth of losing the family home.

Suffice to say he was really in the sh*t financially and looking back it's a miracle that he was able to claw his way back to the freedom and contentment that he enjoys today.

The impetus to write this book came from wanting to share his story with his children. He did not want them to make the same mistakes that he had made and so the book started out as a set of guidelines for them to follow, a kind of road map to a much easier financial life than he had experienced from his late teens, all the way to beyond his 50th birthday.

As his thoughts developed and the ideas evolved he realised that the story he had to tell, and the help and guidance associated with it, potentially had a much wider audience than his own kids. He could help a lot more people. With the benefit of the experience of his own financial journey he had a wealth of knowledge that could enable him to help other people avoid the same financial mistakes, and steer clear of the traps that he had fallen in to. By using the techniques he outlines over the following pages you will find out how he does things differently now, and how he would start out doing things if he had his time again.

By reading this book, if you are not already in some sort of downward financial spiral you will be better equipped to avoid it, and if you are already in some trouble then you will find plenty of suggestions to help you find your way out of it.

Dedication

This book is dedicated to my children.

My hope is that by reading this book and implementing the suggestions made, that they will never have to face the financial challenges that I faced for the greater part of my life.

Acknowledgement

When things were at their worst for me both emotionally and financially, a dear friend and his family offered me help. It was not direct financial help, although this would have almost certainly been offered had I asked. It was emotional support and a place to stay.

I had been forced by my financial circumstances to return to the UK from the country in which I had been living, and was looking for a way to get back on my feet. I had little money, having spent the last of it, probably on a credit card, on the trip back.

I did not really know where I was going to sleep, and at that time I had no work.

The first of these problems was solved by my friend and his family. There is no need to name them, you know who you are.

I will never forget the kindness and understanding you showed and it is to you, in large part, that I owe the fact that I was able to rebuild my life.

Who should read this book

If you are struggling to understand how to live within your means. If you want to get a sense of how you might best use the money that you make. If you want to know what your options might be in terms of sensible expenses, savings, investments, property, cars, then this book will certainly get you thinking. No matter what your current situation, whether you are in debt, want to learn how best to stay out of it, or whether you just want to get some ideas about how to manage your money, this book is for you.

Over the following pages you will benefit from the experience of my own financial journey; from being extremely naive about money; from not actually thinking money was that important; from accumulating a mountain of debt; to having people knocking on my door wanting to remove my possessions, through to finally feeling completely comfortable with the financial side of my life and the way I manage my money. That continual feeling of financial peril is now thankfully only a distant memory.

If you want to learn how to save money by buying things cheaper in terms of day to day spending, then this book is not going to give you that information. My belief is that buying a cheap beer instead of a slightly more expensive one is not going to help you become financially stable or what most people would consider wealthy. This goes for most of the smaller things you are likely to be buying week to week.

What is going to make the real difference is how you manage the money you make, and having a good sense of the longer term bigger picture. It is how to deal with today, how to manage your money month to month, and what you need to think about in terms of the future that I will try to outline over the following pages.

What this book is / is not about

This book comes from my personal journey of learning how money works and the importance of it. A journey of having no money at all and coming very close to being homeless, to finding a sensible way to manage my money.

This is not a book about work, nor is it about how you can increase your income (although this is almost always a good idea so I suggest you seek advice and guidance on this subject via other sources).

This book is not going to give you any inside knowledge, it does not promise to show you how to get rich and it certainly does not provide any advice that claims to be the secret of success. So if you are looking for a book that promises to deliver answers relating to any of these things then you might be disappointed. This book will not offer any tailored advice specific to your particular income, savings or investments.

What this book will do is outline a framework to help you manage the money you have. No matter how much or how little you earn, the principles put forward over the coming chapters have worked for me and I wrote this book because I think properly implemented they can also help other people. The book will encourage you to put plans and systems in place to better enable you to save and invest money, and it will outline a framework and provide some resources to help you do this.

It will also suggest that you start to think about money in a particular way which will fit within this new framework, and help lead to the financial freedom that most people are looking for. Particularly if you are young, have no or at least little debt, you are in a perfect position to start managing your money in a way that will set you up for the rest of your life.

If you are already in a financial mess, then I hope that what you learn over the coming pages will allow you to get back to a stable situation where you once again have control over your money, and therefore better control over your future.

CHAPTER ONE

We live in volatile times

Life was very different for my parents from a financial point of view. They may not have had much money, been earning so much, or had the availability of the things we take for granted today, but the relative cost of the things they required to live; a roof over their heads, food and heating, was a lot lower, relative to earnings, than it is today. For some reason the human race, or at least those in the West mostly, have allowed this to change in a dramatic way which means that for my kids, and probably the generations to come, things are going to be very different.

Therefore managing the money you have, no matter whether you are rich or poor is going to be that much more important.

Let's just get something out of the way before I go on. If you live in the UK, anywhere in the EU, the US or any developed country then on the whole no matter where you are financially you should consider yourself well off. It might be a slightly controversial thing to say but even if you are sleeping on the streets and without a job you are in a better place than many in other parts of the world, you have options, albeit somewhat limited by our circumstances. Certainly if you have a house but still consider yourself poor then think again. You do not actually 'need' anything. You might 'want' things, you might even want to be able to afford a bigger house, a better car, the latest TV, more exotic holidays, better food - but let's be honest, you 'need' nothing!

In other parts of the world people are facing decisions that can mean the difference between life and death on a daily basis. They 'need' things, but most are not in any position to afford them - ever - do not forget that!

That said, I am going to continue to use the word 'need' throughout this book, but understand that I am using it in the way that people in any developed country have come to use it. However, you will now know that when I say I bought a flat screen TV because the family 'needed' to be better entertained, what I actually mean is we wanted it and had saved enough money to pay for it.

Depending on how old you are, how you manage your money will determine the comfort you enjoy, the holidays you are able to take and the things you get to own whilst you are on the planet. If you are young, debt free and just starting out in the world of work, or even still studying then you are in the best place to take advantage of the information in this book.

If you are already slaving away for an employer, or have started your own fledgling business then you too can benefit from the framework and ways of thinking about money laid out over the coming pages.

Even if you are already heavily in debt and can see little opportunity to change this situation in the future then read on. I was in that place but the strategies and procedures I eventually put in place helped me claw my way back from the very brink of financial and family ruin to where I am today, which I can tell you is a much happier place.

I am not a financial adviser and I am certainly not suggesting that by following the framework outlined in this book you will enjoy wealth and happiness forever. The procedures and systems that I eventually implemented helped me, and I willingly tell my story in this book in the hope that others can benefit from my experiences.

Whether you are lucky enough to be a high earner, or struggling on the minimum wage the principles are the same even if the sums involved may be very different. As you make more money new opportunities open up to you. You can choose to save or invest more. You can even buy better financial advice and hopefully build your wealth, and plan for your future in a more structured way.

However, if you are not there yet, but want to start out on the right path in order to give yourself a fighting chance of becoming financially independent, or dare I say it a high net worth individual (more on that later in the book), then I hope that the information and the simple framework I lay out in this book will help in whatever small way to get you there.

Make a plan

A life plan - a financial plan

Having no money is not much fun. Even people with a good job, earning a reasonable salary can regularly find themselves with hardly any 'spare' money at the end of each month. It's demoralising. If you are struggling every month just to meet your family's basic needs it wears you down and contributes to you making what often turn out to be bad financial decisions.

This book is going to help you navigate away from the danger of this situation. With the help of some simple strategies and adoption of a more structured, yet flexible approach to managing your finances. The information in this book will give you a good chance of, at worst staying financially afloat, but I am hoping may even help you get to a point where you can call yourself comfortable financially, or even 'wealthy' - whatever that might mean to you.

If you are already in financial difficulties you are very likely feeling pretty desperate, looking forward to nothing but continued stress and probably quite a bleak future, but hang on. There is hope. There are strategies you can put in place to sort things out and get you to a point where you are able to start building your financial future for the better. The principles and ways of thinking that I outline are in fact very simple, but I am not aware of anywhere that these ideas are generally discussed. Most people get left to make mistakes and find out for themselves, by which time things could be pretty bad.

I am sure if you ask 10 people how they manage their money you will get 10 different answers. What I outline in this book is really my own personal financial journey, and the things I have done that made a difference to me. I have made all the mistakes possible, and probably a few nobody else has even thought of. I was in deep, deep trouble. I once owed a significant amount of money, I had mortgaged a property that belonged to a relative (who was still living in that property), and I came very close during one particular period to losing it.

This went on for years. I lived from day to day, week to week, month to month. I was self-employed so my income was hard to predict and always irregular. Added to this I kept jumping from one thing to another career wise so never really gave myself much of a chance to build anything over the long term.

I was into my fifties before I finally decided enough was enough and I needed to get my financial sh*t together. This book is really the story of this (ongoing) journey. What I learnt along the way will hopefully help you either set out on the right financial path, or get back on track if you have already swayed.

I always hear a lot of talk about the importance of making a life plan but why is this not actually taught anywhere? It certainly wasn't in my day as far as I was aware. My parents probably tried to give me advice and guidance but if they did I must have ignored it.

It is so important, particularly for young people today to get on the right path early on, especially the right financial path. This is the very best time to do it. I would certainly not recommend to anyone that they leave it until beyond their 50th birthday to do so.

Faced with a toxic mix of evaporating jobs, unaffordable property and rising household and government debt, the future from a financial perspective is likely to look very different from that experienced by previous generations.

The more you can do to prepare for this now the better. The financial side of being on this planet should be an important part of your overall life plan.

See bonus chapter at the end of this book – A plan for each decade.

CHAPTER TWO

My own take on personal finance

Over the years I have come up with my own view of personal finance. I like to keep things simple, so my theories are straight forward and hopefully easy for everyone to grasp. I am not going to use complicated financial terminology in this book, mainly because I do not understand much of it so I am certainly not in a position to write about it. I am going to tell you what has worked for me using the language that I and hopefully you will understand.

The financial world is far more complicated than I have outlined but unless you are really quite wealthy then you are not going to need to understand it until you have more money. When and if you get there you will have learnt a great deal along the way which will have built on the theories that I put forward, and in any case you will be able to afford to buy the advice you really need.

This book is hopefully going to set you on the right path but reading it is no guarantee to riches. All I want to do in this short volume is to show you a framework that I have used that has enabled me to wriggle my way out of what was a very very difficult financial position - to where I am now, which thankfully is a much better place.

My simple take on pretty much the whole financial world, at least the world that the majority of people are going to need to deal with is this; start to think about money and how you use it as either income, expenses, debt, savings or investments.

Over the next few pages I will go into more detail about each which will give you the beginnings of your new financial framework, but by way of an introduction this is what I mean….

If you are lucky enough to have a job then you will have income. Even if you are un-employed if you live in the UK at least then you are most likely getting benefits of some kind so at least for now this is your income.

On any income you will pay varying levels of tax which will depend on your employment status and level of income.

Then come your main expenses - I break them down into *unavoidable expenses* and *avoidable expenses,* and an extra category I call the *grey area expenses* which depending on your point of view could fall into one or the other of the main expense categories.

Then there are savings, broken down into long and short term savings (these are further broken down into more strategic targeted savings that I will come on to), followed by debt and then finally investments.

I deal with each of these in turn over the subsequent chapters so you will get a much better sense of what I am driving at about as you progress through the book.

CHAPTER THREE

Income & bank accounts

The way I thought about and managed my finances changed significantly when I decided to run multiple bank accounts. Each dedicated specifically to income, spending or saving. I created a spreadsheet in which I enter my income whenever I get paid. Remember I am self-employed, I invoice multiple clients, so I might get anywhere from 1 to 20 separate payments into my account each month.

If you have a regular job you may only get paid a single figure each month so your calculations are somewhat easier but the principle remains the same.

I have columns setup in the spreadsheet (see *resources* at the end of the book), each column represents an account I run for the specific purpose / column heading. I set a certain percentage of my income against each of these column headings. I have built the spreadsheet so it is possible to 'tweak' the percentages month to month depending on my circumstances so nothing is fixed, the basic principle remains the same every month but there is some flexibility in it. If I have a particular reason to save more money one month, I can adjust the percentage of my income I set aside to saving. Remember though that doing this will mean I have to reduce a set percentage in one of the other columns to compensate. I can never assign more that 100% of my net income (after tax) overall!

It probably sounds more complicated than it actually is, but using the spreadsheet to calculate everything makes it really easy. Once you get into the habit, it will help you to either get back on, or stay on track financially.

First of all there is income. This is the money you have coming in. Since I am self-employed I have to pay my own tax so I immediately set aside a certain percentage for tax. If you are employed and on PAYE (pay as you earn) you can of course skip this step since your tax is already paid at source. This leaves me with what I have left to spend, and by spend I do not mean I can go out and buy a new TV with this money. I mean this is my net income, after tax, and therefore this is what I can use to pay my bills, go on holidays, save for the future, eat etc.

It is this *net* figure that is now further divided and allocated to the other accounts that I run for specific purposes. Those are, my day to day spending, direct debits, household bills, child savings, child allowance, short-term savings, long-term savings and emergency accounts.

Below is the breakdown of all my accounts and details of how they are actually used.

Income

Your income will clearly depend on whether you have a regular job, are employed or self-employed, have regular or irregular work. Regardless of where you sit within these definitions you will have something that you can identify as income. The way I see it, how you divide up whatever income you have is the key to your financial future. It is for you to decide. I cannot make these decisions for you, but what I will do is give you some ideas and a framework to help you decide. The framework that has worked for me.

Tax

How you pay this will be dependent on your employment status and how much you earn. Some people pay nothing, some pay a lot. If you pay nothing then in theory you are not earning enough to pay tax, if you earn a lot then again in theory you contribute more. That's all fine. I think tax is a good thing and is nothing to be afraid of, neither should you feel cheated at having to pay tax.

If you are employed, then there is a high likelihood that your tax will be taken at source. Meaning it is taken out of your pay packet before you then receive the balance, so you need never really worry too much about it. In fact, at the end of each year there is a good chance you will get a tax rebate - some money back from what you have over paid. Therefore, it does not really need to factor into your saving calculations. I will expand on this later in the book.

If however you are self-employed or for whatever reason your tax is not taken at source then the first thing you need to set aside money for is tax. If you are registered for VAT (Value Added Tax, Sales Tax or whatever the equivalent is in your country) then this also needs to be allowed for but this I count also as a tax so assume when I say put X% aside for tax, then VAT, if appropriate is allowed for in this percentage.

For years I never set aside anything for my tax. At the end of each year, when my tax was due I could never pay it. I always had to 'do a deal' with the tax authorities and pay off what was owed over the course of the year. This meant of course that I was not saving tax for the 'current' year. So when a new year came around, there I was again in the exact same situation. It was a vicious circle. Once you are on this ride it is near impossible to get off. Do not do as I did and make this fundamentally, and frankly really stupid mistake.

Bank accounts

Some people seem to get on perfectly well with just one bank account. I tried for years with just one bank account (mainly because I was unable to open any more) but things got in a mess. It was only when I created separate accounts for each of my expenses and savings categories that things began to get easier.

It was also my mindset that changed, in line with the implementation of my suggested financial framework in the form of separate bank accounts. I suddenly found it much easier to separate out my income and expenses in whatever forms via these separate bank accounts, and I continue to do it to this day even though my circumstances are now very different.

So in order to change the way you manage your money you need to do two things. One is to think differently about how and what you spend your money on in the first place, and the second is to run between 6 and 10 separate bank accounts depending on whether you are employed or self-employed, or whether you have kids or not. It really is that simple!

Distributing your income proportionally according to certain levels / percentages set across these bank accounts will change your life. At least it did mine. Now I will explain how I use the accounts I run, and how my money is distributed across these accounts.

These are the accounts I run.

Income / Business Account - into which is paid all the money I earn. I am self-employed and have several different income streams. I mostly invoice clients for my services and they pay me. The money goes into my income / business account.

From this account I immediately transfer a certain percentage of that income to my **tax account** and some more to my **spending account**, this includes the money I intend to save which I will come on to later. I do not transfer all of my income to the tax and spending accounts however, since I run a business I have legitimate business expenses which are paid for directly from my income / business account. I therefore leave some in the account for this purpose.

Tax Account

Since my tax is not taken out of my income I have to set aside money to pay the tax due in the future. I therefore set aside a certain percentage of my income for tax.

If you are employed and on PAYE, then you can probably skip this step as your tax is already taken at source.

Spending Account

This account receives the main chunk of cash from my overall income and it is from this account that I pay into all my other accounts. This is effectively my net income account, it's what I have left after setting aside my tax and leaving a little in my business / income account. It includes the money I intend to set aside for savings.

The total I transfer from my income account is further divided up from this spending account and distributed according to the percentages I have set to all the other accounts detailed below.

The way I further divide up this 'net income / spending percentage' varies. I try to set a certain percentage for each category at the beginning of each month but may vary it depending the circumstances and the amount of money available month to month. For instance, if I am in a position financially to do so, I might increase the amount saved in my short term savings account because I am aggressively saving for a holiday. Any adjustments I make to the percentage set aside in one category will have an effect on another category, as clearly there is only so much to go around. The total allocated can never exceed 100% overall. So each month I make choices depending on my circumstances at the time.

You have to make your own choices as to how you divide up your income but if you would like to see the way I do it, download the spreadsheets I have created to help calculate the figures in a very easy way. You can do so at the book's supporting web site - see the resources page at the end of the book for details.

Direct Debits Account

Direct debits can be trouble. You should only have them setup on an account if you know you have regular income to top up the account with enough to cover all your monthly direct debits. Incidentally you should know pretty accurately what all your direct debits amount to and therefore you will know how much you need to put into your direct debit account each month.

If like me in the past you do not have a regular income, then having direct debits setup on your account can be dangerously costly. If a direct debit falls due, and there is not enough in the account to cover it, then usually a penalty will be payable. These penalties can be quite high, usually between £10 and £20 depending on the bank. This may not sound much but if you have 3 or 4 direct debits falling due on the same day, and all get returned due to lack of money in the account to pay them, then you could be facing an £80 penalty. So not only do you not have enough cash to pay your due bills via direct debit, you are now £80 overdrawn and need to pay that money back before having any left to pay the bills.

It's a slippery slope so consider your own situation carefully before you setup any direct debits.

Thankfully I am now in a position to meet my monthly direct debit commitments. I know exactly how much they all add up to and I make sure that I put enough money into my direct debit account each month to cover them.

I use this account only for direct debits. These are things like life insurance, car insurance, road tax, house insurance, TV licence and so on. I do not use this account for any spending outside of these regular and predictable bills. I usually try to put a little more in each month than I need, thereby building up a bit of a buffer just in case.

Household Bills Account

Some of my household bills are on direct debit and are therefore paid out of the direct debit account. However, for the bills that are not predictable; like utility bills, gas, electric, water etc. I prefer to receive a traditional paper bill and pay by the due date out of my household bills account.

I put a percentage of my income into this account for this purpose. This account is a current account and has a debit card associated with it. I can therefore use this account to either pay bills via the debit card, or via my internet banking facility.

Child Savings Account

This is clearly only relevant if you either have, or plan to have kids. I use this account to save for their future. In my case I have setup an interest paying child savings account for my younger daughter and pay a regular percentage of my income into this account. My daughter does not currently have access to the money in the account, although she can log in via internet banking and see the balance growing. She is not able to withdraw any money until she is 18 years old.

A number of banks / building societies provide this type of 'ring fenced' savings account designed specifically with young people in mind. I think it's great that my daughter can see the balance growing via an app on her phone and is getting used to the idea of regularly saving. Even though she is not actually putting all the money in herself at the current time she stills feels the comfort of having savings that might be used in the future.

Credit Cards

My 'credit card' account is not actually a physical bank account. It is simply a column in the spreadsheet which gives me a figure based on the percentages I have set relating to which account various proportions of my income go in to. The credit card column, for each income entry gives a figure which I use to pay towards a chosen credit card (or other debt). The card chosen might either be the most pressing in terms of payment date due, the one with the highest balance, the one with the highest rate of interest or any combination of these choices. How you distribute this money is of course up to you, and you have to make that decision based on your own circumstances. There is more on the pros and mostly cons of credit cards later in the book.

Child Allowance / Pocket Money

This is different from child savings (and I do not refer here to child benefit or child allowance paid by the government - this if you get it should either be counted as income, or go directly into your child savings account if possible). In an effort to try and get my younger daughter to understand and appreciate money at a much earlier age than I ever did, I have set her up with her own account. She has a contactless debit card, and an internet banking facility. Some people might argue that since she is still at school it's too early for her to have access to money in this way. I would argue however that she is growing up in what is fast becoming a cashless society and that the earlier she understands electronic banking and sees the effect of spending 'plastic' money on her own bank balance the better.

I give my daughter a monthly allowance. I have a column in my income distribution spreadsheet for this purpose which calculates a figure which I mentally set aside for this purpose. I then pay this money (capped at whatever her allowance is at the time) into her allowance account as a single figure each month for her to do with as she pleases.

When I first did this she pretty much blew the lot as soon as money was paid in. However, as time has gone on, and she has got to understand that the money I pay into that account is all she is getting, she started to treat it a little like a salary. She now knows that if she wants something she needs to make sure that she saves a little, rather than spending everything in the account every time she goes to town.

She does not run all the accounts I outline in this book; she has no need to yet. Importantly though she is starting to understand how hard it is to get money in the first place, how easy it is to spend it, and the importance of saving. She can also transfer some of her own money into her separate savings account which she knows she can only access when she is older.

Short Term Savings Account

My short term savings account is simply a basic bank account with no debit card facility. I can transfer money into it from my spending account, but in order to get money out of it I have to transfer it out to another account via internet banking. This means that day to day it's not so easy to spend money from this account. It's a savings account so I do not want to be doing this anyway. It's for targeted savings so all I really want to use it for is to accumulate money for specific uses later in the year.

You could if you wanted to take short term savings to another level by having dedicated savings account for each thing that you are saving towards. You might have a dedicated holiday savings account, or an account for savings toward new bikes for your children. Whatever works for you. As a minimum I suggest at least one dedicated short term savings account.

Long Term Savings Account

Like the short term savings account you could have multiple long term savings accounts for targeted long term savings. I run only one and that works well for me. Perhaps if I was able to save more then having several may start to work better. You have to take the suggestions I make and tailor them to your own circumstances.

My long term savings account at the current time happens to be an ISA. An ISA basically allows you to earn tax free interest on your balance. You are only able to save up to a certain amount each year in an ISA to get this tax free benefit, but the allowance is quite high and the majority of people at least would probably struggle to save enough to reach this allowance each and every year.

The method you use to keep your long term savings safe is entirely up to you. However, remember that this money is for the future. It's not supposed to be used in the short term so if it's going to be there a while, and to grow every time you add to it then it might as well be earning interest.

There are countless savings accounts open to you as a saver. Some pay very little interest but make it easy to withdraw your money any time, others pay a higher rate of interest but when you sign up to use them you agree to leave the money in place for a set period of time. Usually the longer this is the higher the rate of interest paid. You can of course always get your money out whenever you like (unless the bank folds but then you, along with countless other people will probably be experiencing bigger problems). You will potentially loose the interest paid if you break the agreement by taking out money early. Some accounts also require you to open with or pay in a minimum amount each month. These again are often the higher interest paying accounts.

You will need to look at your own circumstances, study the market and make choices as to what works best for you at the time.

Emergencies

Finally, I have an account which just sits there in the background slowly accumulating cash which is designed for emergency use only. How you determine what is an emergency is obviously up to you. Suffice to say that this is really money that you were never expecting to need and so had not set it aside to any of your other accounts.

It's surprising how quickly even a small, regular amount of money put into this account can accumulate. I never really watch the balance. It's only supposed to be used if all other sources of cash (not including credit cards or loans -

just do not go there!) have been exhausted and therefore you have an emergency situation to deal with.

Your Accounts

How you setup your accounts is entirely up to you and dependent on your own circumstances but here is a summary of what I think is the minimum number of accounts you will require.

Against each account I have also included a % figure. This is the percentage of the spending balance from my overall income that I use to work out what money goes into each of these accounts.

My system is flexible so this % figure might vary from month to month. The figures you see below are the figures I was using for the month during which I was writing this section of the book. Broadly speaking they would stay the same month to month but I might vary some of the entries, particularly on the saving side depending on my circumstances and savings goals for that year.

If you are self-employed

You will need the following

1. Income Account (this is the account all my revenue comes in to - I move **35%** into my tax account, **55%** into my spending account and leave the remaining 10% in the account for business expenses)

2. Tax Savings Account **(35%)**

Plus, I then allocate funds according to the % shown to all the accounts listed below.

If you are employed (you do not need account 1 & 2 - start here at no.3)

You will need the following

3. Spending Account (if you are employed this is the account your salary gets paid in to - if you are self-employed this is the account you transfer your spending allocation in to, which is then further divided according to your circumstances)

4. Direct Debit Account (35%)

5. Household Bills Account (5%)

6. Short Term Savings Account (5%)

7. Long Term Savings Account (5%)

8. Emergency Savings Account (5%)

If you have or are planning on having kids

You will need the following in addition to the above

9. Child Savings Account (this is used for saving for your offspring's future) (4%)

10. Spending Account for your children depending on their age as required. (1%)

I also allocate a further 20% to pay off credit cards (although this does not have its own physical bank account, it's just a column in the spreadsheet. Clearly if you are not running any credit card debt, and well done you if this is the case, then you can set this column to 0% and allocate more to one of your other accounts. If you add up all the % figures from my spending balance allocation, and include the credit cards allocation you will find it all comes to 80%. The remaining 20% is left in my spending account and that is what I use for my own day to day spending.

I have made the spreadsheet that I use to calculate all the income allocation figures available for free download. Go to the resources page at the end of the book for the link.

Setting up and distributing your income across these accounts is the easy bit. It made a huge difference to me but it is not the end of it. Next you have to change the way you think about spending your money and start to make some sensible choices in this regard. Over the next few chapters I will outline my own thoughts on this and hopefully you will begin to see how my overall approach is designed to work.

CHAPTER FOUR

Expenses (spending)

Expenses are what you spend on a day to day basis. The housing costs you are liable for (mortgage or rent), the bills you need to pay, walking around money and so on. I break these down into separate main categories, *unavoidable expenses* and *avoidable expenses*. Then I have a third expenses category that I call the *grey area expenses* that could contain some of the expenses from either of the other two main expense categories depending on your point of view.

Unavoidable Expenses

Unavoidable expenses are, as the name suggests, unavoidable. They are housing costs, council tax, energy bills. To a degree you can decide how much you spend on these things but they will mostly be dictated by where you work, where you choose to live and what suppliers you choose. There are clearly choices you can make to minimise these expenses but nevertheless you will need to set aside an appropriate percentage from your spending balance in order to cover them.

Avoidable Expenses

Some of the expenses which I would consider avoidable, others might consider absolutely necessary. Take a mobile phone as an example. My teenage daughter would argue that a mobile phone is a vital part of being alive and that without one life would surely end. The reality of course is that life would not end. It might cut off a convenient channel of communication for some people but life would go on. It's a nice thing to have, and if you are working and enjoying a regular income then the chances are you will be able to budget for a mobile phone. However, if push came to shove and you needed to cut down on expenses then things in the avoidable expenses category are where you should look to make these cuts first.

Other things that might be in this category are TV streaming subscriptions, magazine subscriptions, interest on debt (accumulated on credit cards - if you do not use credit cards then this is automatically an expense that is avoided), car or transport related expenses. Some would say they need a car for work and this is a valid argument. In which case perhaps car expenses would go into the 3rd expenses category - grey area expenses, or for some, unavoidable expenses.

Grey Area Expenses

Your point of view and particular set of circumstances will determine what spending falls in to this category. As I have already mentioned for some a car is essential, and therefore arguably unavoidable, for others it is not. Likewise, you might consider that eating out or enjoying a coffee in a smart coffee shop now and again is frivolous expenditure. I call it 'having a life money'. Saving pennies is not going to make you rich. Not enjoying your life is going to make you sad, and quite possibly ill. So you have to make your own choices based on your income and what you consider important. Spending money is fine, you need never feel guilty about it providing you have the income to support it.

Another grey area expense for me is insurance. Not everyone needs insurance, at least not all the insurance that might be available. Unless you run a car in which case this becomes an unavoidable expense unless you are prepared to break the law. Likewise, if you have a mortgage then you are usually required by your mortgage provider, to at least have buildings insurance. Even if it is not the case then I would see this as a very sensible and justified expense. The insurances that I am talking about being in the 'grey area' are life insurance, illness insurance, pet insurance, house contents insurance, legal expenses insurance and so on. You can buy insurance for pretty much anything and companies are only too willing to sell you insurance for things you do not really need. You will have to make your own spending decisions depending on your own personal situation.

I have life insurance for instance because I have a dependent family and if anything ever happened to me I want to feel comfortable that they would be OK financially. I probably should have critical illness or income protection insurance for the same reason but I do not have it. Just writing theses lines is making me anxious about not having this insurance which demonstrates how the whole insurance industry is built on fear. Fear of something going wrong that will cost you money.

Insurance is a tricky one. You need some, but it is very easy to be over insured. Look at your options carefully and make sensible choices based on your own circumstances and lifestyle.

NOTE: Some bank accounts provide certain insurance as part of the account benefits. My own account for instance gives me mobile phone insurance, worldwide travel insurance and roadside assistance for my car. Of course you need to check that the cover provided is adequate for your needs and your particular circumstances but it's sometimes worth choosing a particular bank account over another for the benefits that it can provide.

Specific Expenses

I am briefly going to give you my thoughts on some specific expenditure decisions that you are likely to face at least once, if not several times throughout your life. These are expenses relating to the purchase of a house, a car and family holidays or some other kind of adventure.

Property

Everybody needs somewhere to live so buying or renting a house is really an unavoidable expense. It used to be very easy to borrow money to buy a house and as a result lots of people borrowed way more than they could realistically afford and many then got into financial difficulties. Some even losing their house.

When it comes to property take things slowly. For many a house is going to be the most expensive thing they ever buy. Get advice and opinion from everyone willing to give it, and then way it all up and make your decision. This is still no guarantee that things will work out well for you but if you have not done proper research and due diligence then you only have yourself to blame if things go wrong.

These days, with the availability of mortgages far more scarce, and the stringent eligibility checks that are done prior to being offered a mortgage in the first place then there is less that can go wrong.

If you are unable to borrow money to buy a house, as frustrating as this might be there is probably a good reason for it. Take the information as an incentive to improve your finances so you can borrow money for this purpose at some time in the future.

Cars

Most people these days like the convenience of owning a car, and I accept that for many it is an essential purchase, enabling them to get to work and earn an income, have days out with the family, bring home all that shopping!

However, cars are expensive. Not only to buy but to run over the course of their short life. For the most part they rapidly decrease in value, they need to be maintained, they need fuel, insurance and road tax.

I have not actually done the calculation but if I added up all the money I had spent on or relating to cars over the years I think I would be horrified. I have never owned a new car, preferring always to buy used, and mostly older cars because they were cheaper. Even so I still had all the costs that come after you buy a car, whether it be new or old.

My only words of advice are to think carefully about how much money you want to spend on something that will get you from A to B. Particularly if you live in a city, try walking - it's free and for most people good exercise. When you need a car, hire one, or take the bus or a cab. It might seem extravagant to take a cab but you can enjoy a hell of a lot of cab rides for the actual cost of running a car.

Holidays and Adventure

For many the annual family holiday, or several if you are lucky enough, have become the norm. I am not about to tell you that holidays are a waste of money. Quite the opposite actually. For years my family and I went without holidays because of my financial screw ups. Looking back, I now see that I should have better organised my finances so I saved a little every month for these holidays.

It's not because I feel I deserved a holiday or necessarily wanted a tan. It's because my family and I missed out on a lot of adventure. You can own a lot of things, most of which will become completely meaningless to you over time and you will almost certainly forget that you ever had them. Experiences though stay with you. It is the adventures, the challenges, the good and even the bad times of travel that stay with most people so to miss out on this is perhaps not such a good life choice. I will never get that time back again.

That said, save for this adventure. Do not do it on credit because then the memories may not be so much fun!

CHAPTER FIVE

Debt

Some people are comfortable with debt, others not so. If you get into debt with your eyes open and in a strategic way, then for most people it's not a problem. I am talking mainly about buying a house and taking on a mortgage for instance. This is a debt. You borrow what is usually a huge amount of money and commit to paying it back for much of the rest of your life, making monthly payments that are often geared towards fluctuating interest rates. Your monthly payments sometimes go down, often they go up but whatever happens you owe the money until it's all paid off.

Other people get into debt by accident. Of course it's not really by accident, you have to consciously take on and agree to taking on the responsibility of the debt in the first place, but debt can very quickly spiral out of control, become unmanageable and leave you in a very dark place, both financially and emotionally. This was what happened to me.

Debt is not only the money you borrow in the first place, but the interest payable for the privilege of taking on that debt. So in very simple terms if you borrow £500, by the time you pay it back whatever it was you used the money for may well have cost you £750 or more.

There are lots of forms of debt. Mortgages, bank loans, car hire purchase, leasing, credit cards and so on.

Whenever you take on a debt you usually agree to pay back a certain proportion of the debt each month. Small amounts of debt over short periods of time are manageable for most people with jobs. It's when you take on too much debt, or if you miss even a single month's payment on a debt that things begin to go wrong.

I now think of debt this way. Debt is like agreeing to a salary cut. Let's say you earn £2000 a month. You have a bank loan which you have agreed to pay back at £100 per month for 36 months. You also have a credit card and last month you used it to buy a new laptop for £500.

You would like to pay the bank loan and all of the credit card balance but that would leave you only £1400 from your salary, which, together with everything else will mean you struggle to get through to the end of the month. So you decide to pay the bank loan but only £200 of the credit card which is more than the minimum payment due, but still leaves a balance on the account. You now have £1700 from your salary but also have a £300 balance on the credit card, too which will be added interest.

Next month you still have the bank loan to pay but both the gas and electric bill come in and those must be paid. Each one of these is £200 so from your salary you now only have £1500 left before you even consider a payment to the credit card. You decide to only pay the minimum amount on the credit card this month so there goes another £50. Despite this you are now left with only £1450 from your salary so this month is again going to be a struggle.

Interest on the credit card now starts to accumulate. You end up in a situation where each month interest is added to an even higher balance. It's the benefit of compound interest but not in your favour!

A few bad months, some unexpected expenses and a couple of weeks' holiday (booked when things looked better) mean that you decide to take out another credit card to cover all the expenses. How hard can it be to pay it back when the holiday is over and things settle down again at work?

Except that now you have two credit card payments to make. Even more comes out of your salary each month before you even begin, and so on and on and on.

So you see it's really easy for this to get on to a downward spiral, effectively cutting the overall income you have available each month.

Mobile phone contracts are a form of debt, which I think often goes unnoticed by people. You take on a contract, usually for at least 24 months and agree to pay a certain amount of money each month for the phone and the facility to use it. The handset itself can be free or you might even have to pay an upfront amount to get it. In the case of an iPhone for instance, one of the more expensive phones on the market then you will often have to pay perhaps £100 upfront for the handset and then anywhere from £45 to £60 per month at the time of writing. Assuming you have an all-inclusive contract so you pay nothing further for texts or call time, and depending on the actual handset then over the course on the contract the phone will have cost you anywhere between £1180 and £1540. You could have purchased the sim only without a handset and have the same calling and texting deal for around £20 per month. So the 'facility to use element' will have cost you less than £500 over the term. Taking the higher figure (assuming we are talking about an iPhone 6 for instance) this means that the handset has cost you £1040. Currently the price of a sim free iPhone 6 is around £540 - still a lot of money but you are effectively paying £500 in interest when you have this type of phone contract. If you can afford to buy the handset outright, or use an older model of phone that you already own then a sim only option will usually cost you significantly less over the longer term in many cases.

Debt is a horrible thing. Avoid it if you can. Manage it carefully if you take it on.

One more word of warning. The research I did for this book suggested that when people get in to debt, mental and emotional problems can also follow. This happened to me. When you are in this state the decisions you make are never coolly calculated and well thought through. It is really easy to convince yourself that the solution is to borrow more. That paying one credit card by drawing cash from another is OK. That treating yourself to some shiny new, and often expensive item will make you feel so much better and everything in the world will be OK again. NOT true. I have been there, I have done all of those things and it just gets worse and worse and worse. People will warn you that this is the case and you will not listen. Only you can break the cycle. Do not be a debtor, it will ruin your life!

Specific thoughts on types of debt

Mortgage

Getting a mortgage is for most people part of life. It's a milestone in the path through life and in most cases a good thing providing you can afford it. When you are young and just starting out it's likely that getting a mortgage is going to be a pretty scary thing, and it should be. You effectively have to commit to paying a pretty big chunk of change back to the lender every month. Regardless of whether you have work or not, whether you get ill or your circumstances change in another way. You can of course put safeguards in place to mitigate these risks but it will all add to the cost of what is probably going to be quite a struggle in the first place.

That said getting on the housing ladder is for most people a sensible move. If you can make it through the first few years then it will get easier. If you are lucky, interest rates will stay low, your house will increase in value, your salary will also increase and everything will become far more affordable.

Just go in with your eyes open because many people have lost a lot of money in relation to property. Not everyone can be a winner.

I am in no position to be able to advise anyone on the right type of mortgage. There are so many options and the only advice I can give you is to seek advice. Try and learn as much as possible about the market before you agree to anything. It is very easy to think that one mortgage is very like another. They are not. They all offer different rates of interest, different clauses in terms of early re-payment, different setup fees etc. Do your homework.

For example, I learnt something only the other day that I had never known relating to some fixed rate mortgages. Fixed rates are very popular because they allow you to fix the rate of interest you pay for a fixed period of time. So let's say you have a 5 year fixed rate you will know that no matter what happens to interest rates, at least for the next 5 years your monthly payments will remain the same. That's comforting and easy to budget for. Lots of people take that option if they can. I wonder though how many people on fixed rate mortgages know that there is most likely a clause in their contract that means at the end of the fixed term, the lender, if they so choose, can decide not to offer you another fixed, or even variable rate. In fact they can if they so choose demand all their money back and not offer you continued lending on your mortgage - at all - they can effectively force you to try and find another mortgage elsewhere, or sell your house!

It's scary what is in the small print so I suggest you get up to speed and know what you are signing.

Renting

For many people, particularly young people, renting is the only option because there is no way they can save for a deposit on a house of their own. Some people are really comfortable with renting and they somehow manage to get great deals, in wonderful properties with kind, considerate and fair landlords. If you are one of these then well done. You are probably in the minority.

In my experience, like most things it comes down to money. If you do not have much money to spend, have a low credit rating and irregular income then your options are going to be severely limited and you will most likely end up in pretty substandard property with a landlord to match.

If on the other hand you have a good job, regular income and a flawless credit score then things might be different.

Renting is fine. It's a housing cost and although it may not be the same as owning your own property, for some it can mean less to worry about in terms of house maintenance, and more flexibility in terms of the ease of moving from one place to another.

If you were to actually add up what most people pay for a mortgage, including all the interest paid over the long term, then renting might actually not look so bad an option.

As with everything do your research, be patient and try to find a property that suits you at a price you can comfortably afford.

Credit Cards

I write more specifically about credit cards in the next chapter but suffice to say my opinion of credit cards is somewhat influenced by my own experience with them. For many they are a necessary evil. I still use them but I use them very differently to the way I did when I first got one, then two, then three and so on. I think at one point I had more than 10 credit cards, and I know now that this is not at all uncommon!

If you are sensible and can control your own emotional need to own stuff, then credit cards have a place. If you are not this person then avoid them.

Bank Loans

For specific purchases there is sometimes a reason to seek a loan from a bank or building society. Depending on your own personal circumstances this can often be the cheapest form of borrowing. You will of course have to meet the stringent financial criteria that the bank demands in order to qualify for the loan but this is a good thing. If you do not have the income to support a loan, then you should not be borrowing the money in the first place.

Hire Purchase / Lease Purchase

Hire purchase (HP) or leasing is often associated with cars. I personally have never gone down this route but I know people that have and as with most debt under the right circumstances it is fine. In fact, leasing can often provide some tax benefits, particularly related to the self-employed and people running their own businesses. Again do your research. If your circumstances are such that HP or leasing is an option, and you have the level of income to support the payments over the term you agree the contract then fine.

Pay Day Loans

Just do not go there. The interest rates are so crippling that if you make the mistake of taking out a payday loan then I can pretty much guarantee you that things will turn out badly. When things were at the very worst for me financially, even I was sensible enough not to go down the route of payday loans.

Just to give you a very simple idea of how quickly things can spiral out of control. Let's say you borrow £200 from a payday loan company or equivalent. Some of these companies are charging 1% interest per day. This may not sound too bad but believe me this is very expensive money!

By the end of week one, assuming you have not paid off the loan yet you might owe about £214. Now of course interest is accruing on £214, not the original £200 so your interest costs are going up by the day. After a month you will probably owe closer to £260 and if you have still not paid off the loan after 2 months, which given your desperate need for the money in the first place is highly likely, then you will almost certainly owe nearly £350.

You hopefully see now why I strongly suggest that you stay away from this type of debt. Thankfully it appears that the government (in the UK at least) is now looking to ban this type of loan but I don't think it has happened yet.

Do not be the person that uses the services of payday loan companies!

NOTE: There are plenty of other forms of debt, far too many to go into in this book. Suffice to say that the forms of debt outlined above are the ones that most people are going to come up against.

CHAPTER SIX

Credit, debit & pre-pay cards

Credit Cards

Get one, within a few months you are likely to have at least a £1000 credit limit. Go out and spend it all. Buy something that you think you really need. Within about 2 weeks I am going to guess that you will realise that maybe that thing you needed so much was not so important after all. Now there is something else you think you cannot live without, and so it goes on. Now see how long it takes you to pay off the debt you just accumulated for the first thing you 'needed'.

Hopefully for most this little exercise will not be necessary, and if it is it will teach you a valuable lesson early on. Stop buying stuff on credit! It costs you a lot more than it would do otherwise, it takes ages to pay off in most cases, by which time the thing you bought has either broken, has been stuffed to the back of a cupboard or is no longer of any use to you.

Taking a credit card is a bit like making a deal with the devil. They do have their place which I will go in to later but on the whole they are dangerous for most people. Taking on any kind of debt where the interest rate is similar to that of the majority of credit cards is only ever going to end badly for at least one party involved in the deal.

I have not done any formal research on this but it is my suspicion that credit cards are mostly used by the poor, or at least by the not particularly well off, to buy things that they do not really need. In some cases, and this has been true for me, credit cards are used for something even worse. That is to buy food (which I know you do need), or to pay bills. I suspect thousands of other people have even used one credit card to pay off the minimum monthly payment on another credit card, but please do not to be one of them.

If you can steer clear of credit cards altogether then this is far and away the best thing. They do have their place, but they need to be used wisely. My belief now is that you should avoid using credit cards for day to day spending. They should only be used for strategic purchases where whatever it is you feel you need can be purchased and paid off before you buy the next thing you do not need.

In the past I have used credit cards to pay for holidays, effectively paying off whatever balance I had on the card prior to the holiday, and then using it to fund the forthcoming trip. Far from ideal but nevertheless planned and strategic. I know earlier I said never to pay for holidays on credit and this advice still stands. I only mention what I have done in the past in an effort to encourage you not to do the same thing if you can avoid it.

In any case whatever you use a credit card for, unless you pay off the whole balance at the end of each month (in which case you might as well use a debit card*), then you are going to be paying interest on the balance. In most cases interest on credit cards is very high compared to other methods of finance.

TIP. By all means use credit cards, do not have too many and never have them in your wallet. Use only for strategic and planned purchases and work out in advance your plan and time frame to pay them off.

*Using a credit card can provide certain consumer protections that debit cards do not provide. Do your own research here as to what works best for you in relation to what you are planning to buy.

Store Cards

Store cards are a bit like a toxic version of a credit card. They will encourage you to spend more money than you ever planned in a single shop! Just do not get them.

Debit Cards

Debit cards are OK in my opinion. What you spend on a debit card comes directly out of your bank account at the time of using the money. This means that you know where you are and can only spend the money you have. However, what I would suggest is that you heed the advice outlined earlier relating bank accounts. This way you will have already set aside money for bills, direct debits and savings to specific bank accounts, leaving whatever is left in your 'spending' account.

You might also hear about charge cards. They are still around but debit cards have effectively taken over where they fitted into the market. The concept was that you used them like a credit card, but paid off the whole balance at the end of each month. The provider of the card would make money on transaction fees charged to the retailer and an annual fee for the benefit of the card charged to you. Take my advice and do not bother with them.

Pre-Pay Cards

I love pre pay cards. They are a relatively new entry to the plastic money products available. I even use a prepay card as one of my short term savings accounts. I top it up regularly with whatever money I have allocated to short term savings then use the card when it comes to needing those savings for things like holidays, weekends away etc. I personally have a prepay card that has a Sterling, Euro and US Dollar facility so this pretty much covers me in terms of the type of holidays I take. I can move whatever money I need from my Sterling card to my Euro or US Dollar card and this then allows me to spend in whatever local currency I need which helps me keep better track of where my money is going and exactly how much is left. No exchange rates to juggle with, except for the initial transfer. You know where you are with pre-pay cards.

CHAPTER SEVEN

Savings

Saving money is often difficult for a lot of people. With the constant stream of bills, a mortgage to pay, council tax, food and so on it's not easy to save anything. Unless you earn more than you actually need on a monthly basis of course. If this is you then great, well done. If like the majority of people these days you are living month to month, then you are going to find saving anything difficult.

For years I saved no money at all. I lived on whatever I made each month, and in fact mostly spent a lot more than I earned which is why I got into a real financial mess from which it was a miracle that I recovered.

Looking back, I really do wish that I had implemented the methods I outline in this book much earlier. Life would have been so much easier. Even if you have very little to save, if you only have £5 a week, even £5 a month, save it. Get into the habit of putting money aside to the various accounts I suggested earlier in the book. As your salary increases you will naturally be able to set more aside but importantly you will have got into the habit of doing so.

I break saving down into two main categories. Short term savings and long terms savings.

I have separate accounts for each of these and every time I get some money in I set aside a certain percentage of that money for each of these accounts. What that percentage is for you will depend on your circumstances but try at least to put some away just to get into the habit of it. It's surprising how quickly even small amounts of money add up over time.

Plus of course there is the wonderful thing known as compound interest. Get comfortable with compound interest. When you are a saver compound interest is your friend. Very simply if you don't know what compound interest is, it's the interest that accumulates on your savings. With interest rates so low at the moment it is never going to be that much but nevertheless it's free money.

To keep the numbers simple as an example, if you save £100, after a year you might earn £10 interest on that amount. Now you have £110 on which interest is paid, which after another year earns £20 interest, so you now have £130 and so on. This is all without you actually paying anything further into the account. That, very simply is compound interest.

Long Term Savings

It is important to save some of your income. I never did when I was younger and I only started saving in my 50's. This was way too late and it is one of the biggest regrets of my life. It was my own fault that I made life very difficult for myself financially due to my failure to save any money. Do not make this mistake. No matter how much you earn, save a little. Even if it is only a few pounds, or even pennies, get into the habit of saving something.

Long term savings are for the future or the much bigger things you might purchase throughout your life. Property, cars, god forbid boats, planes and so on - more on these last two things later.

You need to set aside a certain amount out of your income and save for the long term.

Within longer term savings I would also include unexpected substantial expenses, emergency funding requirements and so on. Perhaps a relative dies unexpectedly and you suddenly have funeral expenses to deal with. Your boiler packs up in the depths of winter. It's nice to be able to draw on some savings to be able to deal with this situation without having the worry of how to fund it all, or worst of all, needing to resort to using credit cards.

Short Term Savings

There will always be things that you need to save money for in the shorter term. Annual holidays, weekends away, car servicing bills etc. These are expenses that you typically expect to have every year and if you set aside an appropriate amount from your income then you will be in a much better position to be able to deal with them when the money is needed.

Targeted Savings

I know some people swear by targeted savings. Meaning they know what they are saving for and they save specific amounts for each thing each month. Often this can mean putting money into separate accounts until the savings goal is reached, and then you can go out and buy it. This was always how it was for earlier generations, except they perhaps put cash into separate jars. They never really had the availability of credit in the way we have today and the reality of debt meant a very different thing to them than it does for us today.

Personally I just put all my savings into the various savings accounts I run within the long term and short term saving categories I have defined. This works for me. These days I have realised I do not need to buy many more things to clutter up my life, but I had to buy a hell of a lot of stuff that turned out to be rubbish before I came to this conclusion. I am not going to kid myself and think that I can tell you that you do not really need to buy most of the stuff you are convinced you need, it's something you just have to find out yourself.

Child Savings

I treat these separate from my own savings. Having been lucky enough to have children I consider it my responsibility to not only provide for them during the period of growing up, but also to provide a 'leg up' no matter how small this might be in the future.

I want to be able to help in those difficult early stages of independent life so I regularly save for this purpose. I do not put an enormous amount aside but just a little whenever I receive income. Over the period that we are usually talking about this adds up to a sizeable chunk of cash that is likely to come in very useful indeed.

It is important to note here that my own personal view is that if you give someone a leg up this is good and usually enough. It is also important however to instill the knowledge and ethic to enable your children to earn their own keep, and pay their own way.

Emergency Savings

No matter how diligent your planning and financial management, sooner or later there will be a financial emergency that you did not see coming. It might be the death of a family member, emergency repairs to your property, a catastrophic engine failure with your car requiring a replacement. Who knows, that is the nature of emergencies.

For this reason, I have an emergency savings account. Again a small percentage of my income goes into this account on a regular basis and it slowly builds up without me really noticing. Thankfully, at least at the time of writing, I have not had to use it. However, when the need arises I know I am going to be very glad of it. It may not be enough for the particular emergency at the time, but this together with the other regular savings I set aside will at least go some way towards easing the pressure.

CHAPTER EIGHT

Investments

Investments are always a bit of a grey area, and often a bit of a mystery to a lot of people. Investment basically means buying something, 'investing' in order to make a future profit. So the theory being that what you buy is worth more when you come to sell it than it cost you to buy in the first place.

The problem for most people is they do not have enough money to invest, enough that makes a real difference that is. You really need be reasonably wealthy to have enough money to invest for real growth, at least the potential of real growth. Few returns are ever guaranteed!

So perhaps this chapter should really be encouraging you to find ways to increase your wealth before making any suggestions about investing. That said I will go on to give you my take on the world of investments and offer some suggestions relating to what you might consider when carrying out your research in to where to invest your money.

Before I go any further it's worth pointing out that if you are carrying any debt, particularly credit card debt then you should pay this off before putting any money into investments. The reason being that with interest on credit cards often way above 20% you are going to be hard pressed to find an investment that can consistently return anything like the interest you are having to pay on your credit card debt. Paying the debt down first is an investment in itself.

Traditionally investments have been pensions, shares in the stock market either purchased directly or through unit trusts administered by an investment fund, usually handled for you by a large company who specialise in making these investments for you (for which you usually pay a sizeable fee incidentally).

However, at the time of writing things are looking pretty bleak as far as pensions and stocks and shares are concerned, at least for the smaller investor. By the smaller investor I mean someone without 10's of thousands of pounds to invest. With interest rates at as good as zero, and serious talk about the likelihood of negative interest rates then putting your money into a pension or stocks and shares may not be the best choice for you at the current time.

That said it is vital that you do plan for the future in terms of investing some of what you earn now, in fact more than some, as much as you can, into a range of things that have a pretty good chance of returning more than you put in at some time in the future, or at the very least keeping pace with inflation.

Due to the financial climate this makes the choice of where to put your money very difficult. You could put some into a traditional pension. This is relatively safe at least but unlikely to grow into a big pot of cash. Other investment possibilities might be property which over the last couple of decades has proved to be one of the best investments for those lucky enough to be in a position to jump on the ride.

It is not my intention to tell you exactly what to invest in because everybody's circumstances are different and depending on how much you have to invest, the risk level you are comfortable with and the time between making the investment and when you are likely to need to cash it in will determine what is a sensible course of action for you.

This is an area where you should get proper financial advice. I am only suggesting to you that you need to take investing in your future seriously and plan for it accordingly. How you do this will be down to you and your particular circumstances.

Making investments for the future is necessary but with pensions and stock and shares not giving the returns they used to then it could be time to look at alternatives (making different spending choices can also be a form of investment). I tend to think a little out of the box, and I am a comfortable non-conformist, so while everyone is investing in safe, but low return options I look to see where else I can put money. (Just not all of it!)

These are not always the safest ways to invest so I am not suggesting you follow the course I take but at least for some of your cash then there is no reason why you cannot look at these types of alternative investments.

Classic cars. A volatile route, you can lose all your money if you are not careful, but with the right research and sensible choices then if you need to run a car you might consider a classic car. Buy the right classic car then not only can you enjoy it while you own it, it is probable that it will increase in value, or at the very least not plummet in value as a new car would. It's not likely to be a huge increase but at least if you can sell it at more than you paid for it then it will have proved to be an investment. (You should of course factor in the cost of running this type of 'investment' over the term of ownership)

Property. Buy to let has been booming in the last few years but with the government imposing tougher rules on property investors in an effort to slow the market this may not be such a good investment in the future. That said if you are in for the long term, and you are in a position to borrow the money to get going then land or property is probably still a good choice for many. Bear in mind though that a lot of people have lost small fortunes on the wrong kind of property investments so tread carefully, do your research and do not put all your cash into property alone.

In the past property has not only gone up in value but prices have also sometimes fallen. Often when there is a fall it can be dramatic as this usually means that the market is 'correcting' itself. Many analysts suggest that we could be approaching a property crash, or correction, quite soon. This is based on the fact that historically, when the average earnings to property price ratio gets to a certain number then a property price crash has followed. When things are stable and the market is working as most people believe it should, then that multiple should be about 3 - 3.5x. Meaning that if you multiply the average salary by 3.5 then you should get a figure that would buy you a house. However, at the time of writing the multiple required to buy even a starter home in many parts of the country is more like 6.5 x average salary. This is regarded as well towards the danger zone.

Overseas Property. Trickier but still viable under the right circumstances. In my experience property in other countries rarely goes up in value in the same way as has been the case in the UK, at least in the short term. That said this is not necessarily a reason to avoid investing in property overseas. If you can buy the right property and make it pay for itself in terms of producing a rental income when you are not using it then it might well be a good option and you can enjoy the investment yourself sometimes as well. Just be sure to consider how easy or difficult it might be to sell when the times comes to do so.

Art. Buy a lovely picture and put it on your wall. It may not be everyone's first thought when it comes to investments but art often goes up in value. Not all art of course, in fact most art does not go up in value. As with anything investment related you must do your research and buy wisely.

There are countless other more unusual investment opportunities so I suggest you investigate every avenue. Be careful not to get taken in by scams. As the old saying goes 'if it looks to good to be true then it probably is'.

Yourself. Investing in yourself is very often one of the best investments you can make. What I mean by this is spending money strategically to give yourself a better chance of making more money in the future. Improving your skills with a view to potentially increasing your salary, making yourself more employable and often as a result a more interesting person, are all good things to look at and should be regarded as sensible investments when backed up with the right research and planning.

There are a number of things that are pretty much guaranteed to cost you money so avoid them. As the late Felix Dennis suggests in his book 'How to Get Rich' - 'If if flies, floats or f**ks, rent it'. You will almost certainly lose money if you buy then sell a plane, the same with a boat. However, if you can afford to buy these things in the first place then losing a bit of money when you come to sell them may not be such a problem for you. As for the last one then this is a contentious issue but suffice to say that if your marriage breaks up then both parties will almost certainly loose out.

Start planning for your future as early as you can. Make investments according to your circumstances and what you want to get out of life in your later years. It's likely that not all your investments will provide the return you had hoped for but if you can at least avoid losing big chunks of cash by making sensible and considered choices then you will have achieved more than most.

CHAPTER NINE

Net Worth

If I was asked the question 'What's the most important thing you cover in the book'? It would be this - NET WORTH.

I have not gone into detail about it before now as for most people, until they have put everything else covered in the book in place; organised their bank accounts, paid down their debt and got things set up with a view to their future, then net worth is not really something that has any relevance. However, if there is one thing you should take away from this book, it is to think about your net worth. It's your net worth that is going to make the difference in the future, so the sooner you can move your focus to building your net worth the better.

Net worth, if you have never heard the term before is basically a calculation based on everything that you own of any value, minus everything you owe in terms of debts or other liabilities. In theory your net worth is what you would be left with in cash if you were to sell everything you owned and paid off all your debts.

You have probably heard of the term 'high net worth individual' - your mission, should you choose to accept it is to become one of them!

Keeping a running total of your net worth is a good indicator of your financial health at any one time. It's worth having in your mind since it makes sense to consider how every financial decision you make may impact your overall net worth. Ideally every financial move that you make should be aimed at increasing your net worth.

You should be looking to increase your assets (what you own) and decrease your liabilities (debts) over the course of your life. If when it comes to making a financial decision you consider that a good financial move will increase your net worth, a bad one will decrease it - keeping this in mind will help you focus and determine whether you are about to make a good or bad decision.

It's also worth watching your net worth as it grows / decreases over time. Comparing either on a monthly, quarterly or annual basis to see how your net worth changes over time will help you see the impact of any financial decisions you are making.

You can make the calculation as simple or as complex as you like. I prefer to keep things simple so I really only record the major things in terms of assets or debts. Some people however like to keep track of things down to a much finer detail, the balance of cash in every bank account they run, even if it's only a few pounds or dollars, the value of their 10 year old bike etc. It's really for you to decide how far you go with it, what you track and what you leave out as too small to include.

Changing your focus from the balance in your bank account, to your overall net worth will change the way you consider any financial decision you need to make and will be one of the best moves you make over the long term.

Another way to look at this is to think about how you would like to spend your later years. Assuming you retire and want to live comfortably for another 30 years or so on the savings and investments that you have made, then let me give you some figures that you are probably going to find quite startling. It used to be that the recommendation during retirement was to take no more than 4% out of your savings each year (this could be savings in cash, your pension pot, whatever you have set aside for your retirement). That was bad enough but the figure has now had to be revised due to the financial climate and 'new' rates of return on savings. Now the recommended figures are more like 3%, with some analyst suggesting figures as low as 2.5%.

What this actually means is that roughly speaking for every £10,000 you want to take out per year, you will need about £400,000 in savings. You can of course add your state pension to this if you are eligible for it. This will add another £8000* or so but what kind of retirement are you going to be able to enjoy on only £18,000 a year, and that is if you have the £400k in the first place!

Ideally everyone needs to work to increase their net worth over the course of their lives so that they end up with a fully paid for house and a significant amount of savings. This is what you are going to need for a realistic chance of a financially comfortable retirement.

On the resources page you will see a link to the supporting web site of this book where you can download the simple net worth calculator that I use which will allow you to track your main assets and liabilities on a quarterly basis.

* *Approximate figures - correct at the time of first publication.*

CHAPTER TEN

Tax & inheritance planning

When it comes to tax and inheritance planning you are best advised to seek specialist help as everybody's circumstances are going to be different. The reason I have included a chapter on this subject is simply to draw your attention to the importance of it and highlight the fact that it should be part of your long term financial calculations and life plan, especially if you have children.

If you are employed and pay your tax via PAYE, then you have less to do in this regard. However, if you are self-employed or become a director of a company then how you structure your business will have an effect on the amount of tax that is due on anything you take out of it. Likewise, when you come to sell the business you will pay more or less tax based on how the company is structured. This is certainly something that you need to take advice on from a suitably qualified person, usually an accountant with experience of corporate structures and corporate law.

As for inheritance tax this is also something you need to be thinking about as your net worth grows over the course of your life. If you want to leave money to your kids or other family members in the most tax efficient way, then make sure that you get up to speed with the laws in place at the time and seek the best advice you can afford to ensure that your money is distributed in the most appropriate way to the people that you most want to benefit from it.

For instance, at the time of writing it is possible to 'gift' up to £325,000 to each of your children tax free, as long as you do it while you are alive, and that you survive for at least 7 years after gifting the money. If you are lucky enough to have this kind of cash swilling around, and you want to leave it to your kids, then it makes good sense to ensure that you are up to speed with all these little rules and plan how you are going to distribute your wealth well in advance of the day when you will not be in a position to care any longer.

There are countless other rules relating to tax and inheritance planning, so seek advice from an accountant or a suitably qualified financial adviser and make sure that this side of your financial plan is carefully structured.

CHAPTER ELEVEN

Credit score

I never used to worry too much about my credit score. In any case it was just about as bad as it could have got without me having actually been made bankrupt. It meant that whenever I needed credit for any reason I was never going to get it, and this did not necessarily always relate to borrowing money.

As I got older I realised just how important a good credit score was, and that not having a decent rating was limiting my financial options, and therefore the way I could lead my life a great deal.

For years I struggled with a low credit rating and this meant my options for mortgages were severely restricted. I could never get any car finance, or indeed pretty much any form of credit. I know in the earlier part of the book I have been trying to put you off the idea of credit, but there are times when you will need it. As long as it is strategic and planned, taking account of the potential impact on your net worth then some credit is fine.

Due to my credit score the options available to me were limited in terms of where I could live and the type of property I could buy or rent.

In the past, for a period when I was renting property I was unable even to consider properties available through agents due to the fact that they would have to carry out a credit check on me which I knew would advise them to steer well clear.

My only option was to go to a private landlord of which there are far fewer, meaning of course the property selection on offer is that much smaller.

It was horrible. Once your credit score gets damaged it can be months, even years before it can be 'clean' again.

Look after your credit score. Consider the impact of any financial decision you make.

You can get to see your credit score for free at https://www.noddle.co.uk/

CHAPTER TWELVE

My financial set of rules

Below are a simple set of rules that I try to adhere to and that I encourage everyone to consider.

When I implemented what I have outlined in the previous chapters my life changed. As soon as I could see where my money needed to go, and how much of it was going to one place or another it all made sense. I could see that as long as I kept to the plan, and that I distributed my income according to the plan, then everything would be OK.

However just putting your cash into separate bank accounts is not the only thing that will make a difference to your financial future. You have to get smart about how and where you spend your money and the set of rules I list below has helped me stay focused in this regard.

They will help you either set out on the right financial path, or work towards getting back on it.

The Rules (in no particular order of importance as they are all important!)

- Spend less than you make.

- Setup specific accounts for income, day to day spending, household bills, direct debits, long term, short term and emergency savings.

- The only real way to become wealthy (unless you inherit a fortune) is to find ways of increasing your income (investing in yourself).

- Change your focus from worrying about what's in your bank account month to month to the value of your net worth.

- Keep a running total of your net worth and use it as basis for every financial decision you make. If the decision is likely to result in a decrease of your net worth for any length of time, it is probably not the right move.

- When it comes down to it, there are only two ways to effectively increase the money in your pocket. You can either spend less money or find ways to earn more.

- Do not worry about money you have already spent. It's too late. You will never get that money back no matter what. If you realise it was a mistake, learn from it and make sure you do not make that mistake again.

- By all means use credit cards, do not have too many and never have them in your wallet. Use only for strategic and planned purchases and work out in advance your plan and time frame to pay them off.

- If you have more than three plastic cards in your wallet you probably have a problem. Most people need only two, a debit card and a pre-paid card. Unless you are self-employed when you might have an argument for three, the third being a company payment card.

- Avoid using your savings to finance your consumption.

- It's kind of a nice feeling to be able to pay your bills, set money aside so you always can.

- Do not go 'shopping' unless you have something specific that you need to buy. If this is the case go, but just buy that one thing. Otherwise I guarantee you will spend money on stuff you did not know you 'needed' until you come across it in the shop!

- More income = more options.

- More savings = more options.

- More options = less stress.

- Know your worth and charge for your time. Do not get into the race to the bottom on price. Deliver quality and charge appropriately for it.

- If you are struggling to pay the rent it's difficult to be creative, you are in survival mode, and this clouds all the decisions that you make.

- Remember that time is not money, no matter what anyone says. Time is far more important than money. You will never get back time, once it's past, it has gone forever. Do not waste time. Wasting money or getting into serious debt I can say from experience will end up with you wasting your limited time on this planet.

- Save more than you spend.

CHAPTER THIRTEEN

A plan for each decade

Below is an outline of what to consider, and what you should be aiming for in the 5 main decades of your life, where you are most likely to have earning, and therefore saving potential. You should really start to think about this before you start to earn anything but many people fail to do this and only come in mid way though a later decade of their life, therefore making things that much more difficult for themselves. So what follows are the main things to be thinking about and planning for over the course of your life, starting from about age 10!

Decade 1. 10 – 20 yrs.

Is this not a little too early for financial planning I hear you say? Not in my view. It's a perfect time to start thinking and learning about money, getting into some good habits and looking to the future, with little risk involved at this stage of your life. I would guess that at least for most kids of 10 they are going to have plenty of other distractions that are going to mean that their main focus is way off money or planning in any way for the rest of their lives. I therefore think that it's the parents responsibility to educate, inform and encourage their children to think about savings, investments, the concept of compound interest and even net worth. It does not have to be done in a formal way, it can be made to feel exciting, challenging and even something to look forward too.

If you are already reaching the end of this decade and your parents where not enlightened enough to tell you about these things then it's time to get busy with it yourself. Educate yourself about money and finance. Read up online, talk to wealthy people and garner their guidance and advice. Do not be afraid of money, but learn to treat it with respect and take things slowly when making any decisions relating to it.

As soon as you start working you should very quickly get into the habit of saving. It need not be much at this stage of your life but some at least and more if you can. The more you save now the easier things will be as time goes on, and the more time your savings will have to grow.

During this decade, at least the later part of it anyway is also the time you should be starting to look to the future. You are about to embark on what will hopefully be an amazing life. Start to think about what you want to get out of it and outline your own rough plan of where you think you want to be and when. Much of what you plan will have a direct association with money, how much of it you are making, and most importantly how much of it you learn to keep.

Decade 2. 20 – 30 yrs.

By this time, if you are not in continuing education

relating to your chosen profession then you will hopefully have found a job, or even created one for yourself. It will probably not be paying a great deal at this time since you are in the very early stages of your career.

No matter what you are earning, start an emergency fund. This is really one of the most important things to save for. If anything does happen that means you are unable to earn a salary for a while, then this fund is going to be your lifesaver. By the end of this decade should be looking to have accumulated between 3 and 6 months of your take home salary in this fund.

It's easy to think that when you start earning a salary that all the money you get each month is to be used for the sole purpose of going out and having fun. That's what being in your twenties is all about isn't it? Well yes it is and I am not saying do not go out and do this. Just do not blow the lot. Save some. Save as much as you can in fact because if you have taken the steps outlined in decade one, then you will be fully up to speed with compound interest, and hopefully be quite excited about the fact that money put into a savings account will accumulate more money over time, even if you do not add any more to it (you should of course continue to add to it anyway).

A pound saved when you are in your 20's will be worth more to you in your retirement than that same pound saved in your 30's due to the effect of compound interest. In your 20's, when you are most likely to have fewer responsibilities than in later life (no kids, no mortgage, no or hopefully at least little debt) is the perfect time to be squirrelling money away for later. If you have planned it, and understand why it's important, then it should be a pleasure to be doing it.

Also during this decade you should be aware of your credit score. Everything you do financially should be with your credit score in mind. You need to constantly strive to improve it as not long from now it will be one of the main factors between you getting a mortgage or not.

You might need to take out some credit to help you improve your credit score. It's crazy I know but people with no history of having borrowed any money will have a lower credit score than those with this history. So for this reason alone it's fine to get a credit card. Just make sure you manage the credit carefully, keep the amount of credit you take on low, and always make sure you pay your bills on time or it will have the opposite effect and lower your credit score.

As well as building your emergency fund you need to also set aside money for other savings, one of which might perhaps be a deposit for a house by end of this decade. It will seem daunting but it must be done. As I referred to earlier if you know why you are doing it then hopefully you will feel good about it.

Opening an ISA is usually a good idea at this time, paying perhaps a percentage of your salary in to it each month. This decade is also the time you should be thinking about other smart investments and being open to the opportunities when they arise and you might also look to start a pension. That said at the time of writing pensions are not giving great returns.

Depending on your situation this is usually the decade that might require you to start to think about insurances – life insurance, critical illness insurance etc. Clearly far more important if you get married and plan to have kids but nevertheless worth thinking about even if this is not the case.

During decade one you did of course become fully conversant will all things financial, but it's important not to just sit back and think you already know it all. Continue to educate yourself about money and finance. Things change, opportunities arise, recessions hit. Keep on top of all of this.

Decade 3. 30 – 40 yrs.

For many people this decade is when they are at their height in terms of earning potential. You have hopefully progressed in your chosen profession and your salary reflects this. You may have even started a business in decade two and having now had time to grow you are at the top of your game.

With more money in your pocket this is when the main growth opportunities will present themselves. You should be looking to grow your income even further but importantly with the extra money you have available you should be aggressively paying down any debt accumulated in the previous decade as this effectively saves you money over the longer term.

Assuming for some lucky people it's about this time when they will be in a position to buy a house, then obviously this for most means borrowing the money and taking on a mortgage. Try though when you take on a mortgage that you do so without too many other liabilities to deal with as well. In any case, if you have too many you are not likely to be offered the mortgage in the first place.

As soon as you have a family, assets of any kind, a mortgage etc, it's now time to make a will!

With the other commitments you are likely to take on during this decade then it's easy to forget about that emergency fund. It's also important if possible not to use it to fund the property purchase. The emergency fund is your safety net and all you should be doing with it is building on it. By the end of this decade you should be looking for between 9 and 12 months of take home salary in this fund.

Continue to build other savings and investments and during this decade it's also time to start to pay attention to your net worth. Learn how to calculate your net worth and consider the impact on it when making any major financial decisions.

Decade 4. 40 – 50 yrs.

So you are established. If you have planned properly over the last few decades and luck has gone your way, then things should be going great. You will have fairly sizeable savings, a healthy emergency fund, some other investments for the future and hopefully you will be well on the way to completely paying off your mortgage.

You should be proud of yourself. You are in a great position compared to many other people who did not make the plans or who were not prepared to make the sacrifices you did. Do not screw it all up at this point by taking on any further debt. You started to pay down your debt during the last decade and if there is still some lingering then keep going, but absolutely do not take on any more debt at this time of your life unless you are 100% sure that doing so is going to increase your net worth at some point in the not too distant future.

If you have been employed and on P.A.Y.E over the course of your working career, then the chances are that your state pension contributions will be up to date. However, at this point it's worth checking on the status of these contributions and, if you are in a position to do so, top them up as required.

Decade 5. 50 – 60 yrs and beyond

So this is where the fun really begins. You have a nice little pile of cash, perhaps a house or two, you have enjoyed your life to date immensely, and if you are lucky enough to have your health then you are reaching the time when you can go on and enjoy it even more. You are confident, you have the benefit of experience and now finally realise that what your parents told you was right. The downside is that you might also have teenage kids that like you did, are now saying you are wrong! But that's just life.

Unless you have done exceptionally well then you will probably need to work for another 10 or 15 years at least but this will be on what is hopefully already a solid foundation. Assuming that nothing goes seriously wrong and that you continue to make sensible decisions then things can only get better.

You can start to think about your retirement – Where will you live? Will you be downsizing or consolidating your property or indeed properties in some other way? You can start to think about inheritance planning. What will you pass on to your kids? If you have a business what is your exit strategy and what might the tax implications for this be? These are all great problems to have and by this time of your life you should be able to confidentially deal with them and in fact find them a pleasure.

So that is a very quick and broad outline of what I think are the main things to consider financially over the course of a life.

Here is a quick view of the main points for each decade.

Summary / Checklist

Age 10 – 20 yrs.

Educate yourself about money and finance.

Get into the habit of saving money.

Plan for your future.

Age 20 – 30 yrs.

Continue to educate yourself about money and finance.

Start a dedicated emergency fund.

Set aside money for other savings. ISA etc.

Know your net worth.

Look to constantly improve your credit score.

Age 30 – 40 yrs.

Continue emergency fund saving to reach your target.

Continue to build other savings.

Start to aggressively pay down debt.

Write a will.

Age 40 – 50 yrs.

Avoid taking on any further debt.

Top up NI contributions (if required).

Age 50 – 60 yrs +

Retirement planning.

Downsizing.

Inheritance planning.

Tax planning.

Business exit planning.

Conclusion

So there you have it. A simple set of strategies and some rules adopted that changed the course of the financial side of my life. It worked for me so I see no reason why, if properly implemented and adhered to that it cannot work for you, regardless of the situation you currently find yourself in.

In an ideal world of course this book will be read by young people, who are debt free and just starting out on the path through life. They are the ones that will really benefit from adopting the techniques outlined in the book because they can reap the rewards that much sooner and have more time to build up their savings.

If you are already in deep financial trouble then it's much harder to get out of it, but far from impossible. If this is you then do not give up, there is hope and there is a brighter future at the end of the tunnel. Start to think smarter in relation to money and things will start to change.

Thank you for reading this book and I hope that whatever situation you are in financially that I have helped in some small way to guide you to a more comfortable and financially stress free future.

Resources

Supporting web site

Where you will find more information, my blog and the spreadsheet downloads.

http://financialshit.com

Use the coupon code

freetemplates

To get at 100% discount at the checkout.

Social Media

@financialshit

Free credit Score

https://www.noddle.co.uk

Other Credit Reference Agencies

http://www.experian.co.uk/

http://www.equifax.co.uk/

Debt Advice

https://capuk.org/

https://www.nationaldebtline.org/

https://www.citizensadvice.org.uk/

Banking

I am not endorsing them in any way but I have found it very easy to setup and operate multiple bank accounts with Nationwide Building Society.

http://nationwide.co.uk/

Other banks and building societies are available!

Prepay Card

I am not endorsing them in any way but I have found it very easy to setup and operate multiple currency prepay cards through Cashplus.

http://mycashplus.co.uk

Other Prepay cards are available!

Copyright ©Andrew Turner

Published by Blipp Digital Publishing

www.blippdigital.com

First published June 2016

All Rights Reserved

END

Made in the USA
Monee, IL
05 May 2022